THE LITTLE
TABBY
Cat Book

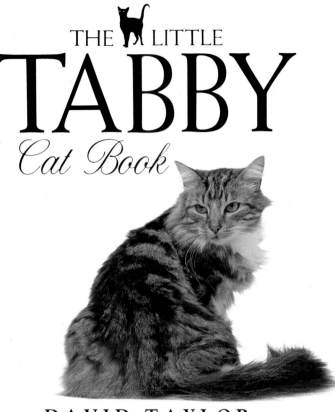

DAVID TAYLOR
DAPHNE NEGUS
Consulting Editor

SIMON AND SCHUSTER
New York • London • Toronto • Sydney • Tokyo • Singapore

A DORLING KINDERSLEY BOOK

SIMON AND SCHUSTER
Simon & Schuster Building
Rockefeller Center
1230 Avenue of the Americas
New York, New York 10020

Simultaneously published in Great Britain
by Dorling Kindersley Limited,
9 Henrietta Street, London WC2E 8PS

PROJECT EDITOR Corinne Hall
PROJECT ART EDITOR Nigel Hazle
MANAGING ART EDITOR Nick Harris
MANAGING EDITOR Vicky Davenport

Printed in Italy by Mondadori

1 3 5 7 9 10 8 6 4 2

Library of Congress Catalog Card Number: 90-32246 [tk]

ISBN: 0 - 671 - 70985 - 2

CONTENTS

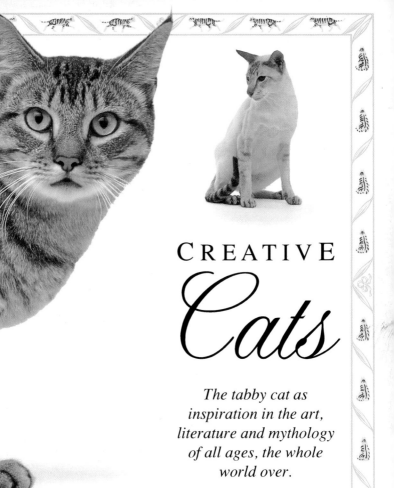

CREATIVE
Cats

The tabby cat as inspiration in the art, literature and mythology of all ages, the whole world over.

FANTASY AND FOLKLORE

Tabby cats have featured in fantasy and folklore for thousands of years. Here are some fascinating felines.

Mice usually come to a sticky end when they encounter cats in fairy stories, and the trusting little mouse in the Grimm Brothers' tale *Cat and Mouse Partnership* is no exception. The two creatures agree to set up house together and buy a can of fat to keep them fed in winter.

TANTALIZED

The cat is tempted by the fat and thrice pretends to be going to a christening, but instead sneaks off for a private snack. When, in winter, the bewildered mouse challenges the cat about the empty can, the cat springs and gobbles up her innocent and trusting friend.

That crafty feline character Puss in Boots has featured in fairytales since the middle of the sixteenth century. French author Perrault published the best-known version of the story in 1697. A miller dies, leaving to his oldest son his windmill, to the second son an ass, and to the youngest son a cat.

CLEVER CLOGS

Clad in the smart leather footwear given to him by his master, Puss in Boots sets off to visit the king. The cat succeeds in tricking the king into believing that his master is a prosperous nobleman, worthy of the princess's fair hand in marriage.

Far Left:
Adventurous Cat;
Left: Puss About to
Be Presented With
the Fateful Boots;
Above: Watchful
Cat and Timorous
Mouse.

Although this is hardly a tale of virtue rewarded, nevertheless all ends well as Puss's master lives happily ever after with the beautiful princess and Puss in Boots himself becomes a great lord. His feline skill has paved the way to great things: a life of success and happiness all round.

NURSERY-RHYME CAT

Pussy cat, pussy cat, where have you been?

I've been to London to visit the queen.

Pussy cat, pussy cat, what did you there?

I frightened a little mouse under her chair.

AMAZING TABBY-CAT FACTS

Cats are a subject of fascination to nearly everyone. Here are some tantalizing tabby-cat facts to whet the appetite.

The domestic tabby is descended from two varieties of wild cat: the African and the European. African cats, which had been quite successfully domesticated by the Egyptians more than four thousand years before, next accompanied the Romans on their extensive sweep through Europe, and met their furry European opposites.

LATIN LIAISON

The kittens had patterned, glossy coats with much stronger markings than either of their forebears. They were the ancestors of today's tabby, which is nothing if not an intrepid traveler. Tiger, one such adventurous European kitty, jumped into a wooden crate for a nap on a local German army base where his owner worked.

He woke up having been flown to Northern Ireland. Neighbors clubbed together to pay for his quarantine fees. Tiger was soon flown back home, safe and sound.

FLYING FELINES

Another flying tabby was Jazz, the only animal aboard the first airship to fly the Atlantic. And Cudzoo was a flying tabby who had a miraculous escape. She tumbled from the twentieth story of a lofty Manhattan skyscraper. Fortunately her fall was broken by an awning.

STATIONARY CAT

Once a familiar sight to female travelers to the West of England was Tiddles who, in his day, was the fattest cat in London, weighing a colossal twenty-five pounds.

Left: Domestic Tabby Scenes;
Above: Prime Viewing Position;
Right: Curiosity and the Kittens.

Home for Tiddles was the ladies' bathroom at Paddington Station. He was spoiled by the attendant who fell for his then waif-like charms. Tiddles never strayed far, unlike Gribouille, a French-born tabby, who relocated to Germany when his owners moved house. Gribouille walked back the 600 miles to visit his French home!

HALL OF FELINE FAME

Here are some tabby cats that have graced the corridors of feline fame in history, film and literature.

Film tabbies are often cast in the role of good-guy, tracking down the villain of the piece while also providing steadfast companionship to their owners. In Stephen King's *Cat's Eye*, one such owner is haunted by a poltergeist, that creates complete havoc all around. Suspicion focuses on the pet tabby. Puss eventually clears his name by saving her from the dark forces.

SLEUTHING CAT

In *The Shadow of the Cat*, a fiercely loyal tabby is witness to his mistress's murder and starts out to wreak revenge by cunningly killing off her mistress's murderers as they search for the missing will.

A tabby also has the rather dubious honor of starring in the very first cartoon ever to be awarded an X-rating. *Fritz the Cat* became a cult movie when it was first released in 1972, and starred a streetwise tabby whose outrageous carryings-on left little to the imagination.

POETIC PUSS

Sir Walter Scott, Scottish author, liked to write with his tabby, Hinx, lying on the table beside him. Edward Lear, writer of nonsense verse, was afraid that his tabby, Foss, would be confused by a house move, so had his new villa built to exactly the same layout.

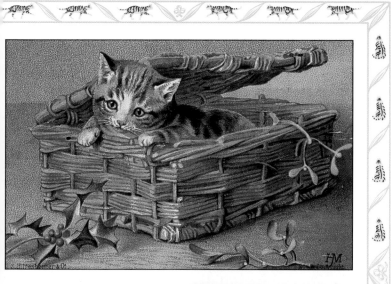

Robert Southey, poet laureate and one of the English Lake Poets, died in 1843 and was most lavishly praised by his contemporaries for his longer poems. He was the devoted owner of a tabby, Dido.

FELINE WRITING COMPANIONS

Thomas Hood, born in London, the son of a bookseller, was another poet of the same era. At one time, it is recorded that he had three tabby kittens, all from the same litter, with the wonderfully original names of Pepperpot, Scratchaway and Sootikins.

Far Left: Fritz; Top: Timorous; Above: Classical Tabby Cat

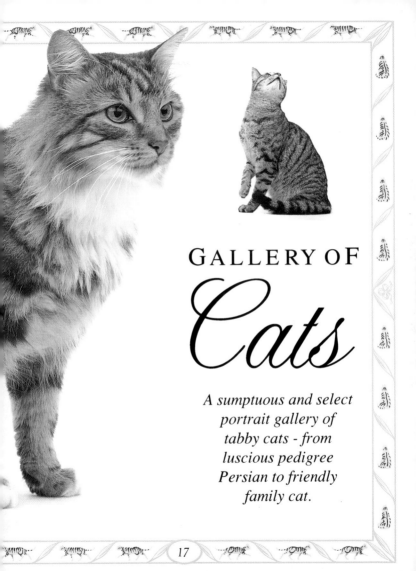

GALLERY OF
Cats

A sumptuous and select portrait gallery of tabby cats - from luscious pedigree Persian to friendly family cat.

FELINE FEATURES

Every cat's features are uniquely expressive of its innermost character. Breeding often shows itself most obviously in the face, and especially in the eyes, the windows of the soul, which are also monitors of the slightest changes in mood, health or well-being. An alert, sparkling, interested cat is a joy to behold, as any cat lover will agree.

OLIVER
Chocolate Tabby Angora

LULU
Exotic Shorthair

HAMISH
Maine Coon

SMUDGE
Chocolate Lynx-point

FLUFFY
Blue Classic Tabby Persian

THOMAS
Non-pedigree

SUKI
Non-pedigree

KREMLIN
Non-pedigree

MAINE COON

It's likely that this breed, the oldest in America, was originally a wild inhabitant of Maine. It is thought that sailors introduced longhaired cats from Europe, and that the Maine Coon was created by crossing these cats with tough farm cats. Popular in the nineteenth century, the breed fell from favor when Persian-fever hit America. It began a comeback in the 1950s.

WINTER WOOLLIES
The Maine Coon has a shaggy coat, burnished chestnut in color with black markings, which is well-suited to chilly winter weather yet feels much silkier than it looks.

WILD SPECULATION
There are those who insist that the Maine Coon's ancestor is the wild racoon. This would in part explain its tendency to sleep in strange positions and odd places. It's a nice idea - but genetically out of the question.

Plumes And Feathers

These cats are large and muscular - they can weigh as much as thirteen pounds - and the thick coat adds to the impression of size. Their tails, which are wide and plumed with long fur, should be the same length as their bodies.

Caracteristics

❧

Affectionate by nature.

❧

Communicates with a pleasing, low "chirruping" sound.

❧

Very fond of human company.

CHOCOLATE LYNX - POINT COLORPOINT

Stream-lined, elegant and decidedly aristocratic, here is a cat with character! These cats are particularly graceful and athletic, with supple bodies and long, slender legs. The long, tapering tail is a very useful aid to balancing, enabling the Siamese to reach the most inaccessible perches with seemingly effortless ease.

JEWEL EYES

One of the Siamese cat's most striking features is its all-seeing blue eyes, that glitter like sapphires and are emphasized by the long, wedge-shaped head.

Perfect Points

The "points" of the breed name are the face and ears, legs and tail. The rest of the body is covered in short, glossy fur the color of pale ivory.

Cateristics

🐾
Exceptionally clever and quick to learn.

🐾
Can be haughty with strangers.

🐾
Will love its owner to distraction.

Attention-Seeker

Siamese cats are known for their temperament, which can be delightful or infuriating - but never dull. This is not a cat that likes being ignored!

CHOCOLATE TABBY ANGORA

The original Angora had its roots in Turkey, where, in the sixteenth century, it basked in royal company. The Chocolate Tabby, however, is not a true Angora. It is a British variety, bred from the Siamese rather than from the original Turkish cat but, apart from having a less strident voice, the differences between the true Angora and the Chocolate Tabby are virtually indistinguishable.

*T*IPPY *T*OES
An elegant mover which trips daintily on petite paws, the Angora keeps its long and bushy tail neatly curled.

CUDDLESOME COAT

The Angora sports a luxuriant coat of fine, wavy fur, with characteristic tabby markings on the face and legs. Its face is framed by a flattering ruff of yet more glorious fur.

CATERISTICS

🐾

Always ready to play and extremely quick to learn.

🐾

A gentle and most companionable cat.

🐾

Delightfully strokable!

EXOTIC LOCATION

Swathed in silkiness and with bewitching, slanted eyes and a small, elegant head, the Angora's forebears must have felt quite at home in the sultan's harem.

EXOTIC SHORTHAIR

This enchantingly snub-nosed cat has soft, velvety fur that's long enough to sink your fingers into. The Exotic Shorthair is a brilliant piece of interbreeding between Persians, American Shorthairs and Burmese. A relatively new breed, which has only been in existence since the 1960s, this cat enjoys excellent health and takes to the show ring quite happily, delighted to show its beautiful self to the admiring crowds.

CALM DISPOSITION
The Exotic Shorthair has a quietly confident, gentle personality and is not easily made nervous.

CHUBBY CHEEKS

Its pretty, full-cheeked face, copper-colored eyes and sweetly snubbed nose make the Exotic Shorthair one of the most appealing cats.

SMOOTH AS VELVET

The Exotic Shorthair is chunkily built, with sturdy, short legs. Its fur, smoothly plush and short, has no feathers or tufts and requires little grooming. The tail tends to be kept low rather than waved aloft.

CATERISTICS

🐈

Intelligent and alert, this cat loves to play.

🐈

A great cat for city-dwellers because its gentle nature is seldom destructive.

🐈

Loving and affectionate, in the best tradition of Persian cats.

BLUE CLASSIC TABBY PERSIAN

This endearing ball of fluff is one of the oldest breeds and had arrived in Europe by the end of the seventeenth century. It has always been far less common than its shorthaired counterpart. The long fur can make it hard to distinguish the tabby markings, which should be deep blue over a bluish-ivory coat.

TOUSLED LOCKS
That delightfully disheveled fur is fine, thick and soft. Desirable markings are laid down in detail for each type, and should be symmetrical.

RARE VARIETY
The Brown Classic Tabby has a compact, stocky body and a short, bushy tail. It is less common than the Blue variety, but equally beautiful.

CATERISTICS

🐾

Not quite as home-loving as most Persians, showing a streak of independence.

🐾

Easy to live with and especially amiable.

🐾

Not in the least temperamental: doesn't suffer from moods.

FURROWED BROW

The faint "M"-shaped "frown line" is typical of Classic Tabbies. Eyes vary from definite orange to a more coppery tone, while nose and paw pads are a charming shade of rose pink.

THOMAS

Thomas's owner picked him out of a litter of kittens because he had such huge eyes and was so fluffy. He was very playful and loved chasing a toy mouse and stalking pieces of wool. But once he was old enough to be allowed out, Thomas moved on to the real thing, hunting and prowling in his local neighborhood.

MIDDAY SNACK

Thomas likes a meal of fish cooked with egg. And he always shares his owner's lunchtime sandwiches.

Taking Fright

For a cat who is such a bold hunter, Thomas can be very timid. He is nervous with strangers and bolts through his cat-flap when he hears them enter the house.

In Retreat

Thomas retreats under the folds of the tablecloth, where he can't be seen: from this safe distance he can observe almost everything!

Cateristics

🐈

Takes a long time to get acquainted, and usually prefers women to men.

🐈

Fond of nibbling on crunchy morsels of toast.

🐈

Wears a collar with a bell, but still manages to pad silently.

SUKI

When Suki was eighteen months old, her previous owner developed an allergy to cats - and Suki had to find another home. Her new owners fell in love with her because she was so pretty, and decided to risk introducing her to their cat Scrabble, a playful young male. Fortunately the two quickly rubbed noses and became the best of friends. Suki is far more sedate than her playmate but occasionally she will agree to a boisterous game of rough-and-tumble or chase.

So Cuddly
Very much a lap cat, Suki is always happy to be stroked and petted and can't get enough affection.

Easy Feeding
Suki's taste in food is decidedly conventional. She turns up her nose at milk, preferring water, and sticks to one favorite brand of cat food: delightfully easy to please!

ACROBATIC CAT

When Suki thinks no one is watching, she lets off steam by racing around the garden, twirling and taking great leaps in the air.

CATERISTICS

Tends to be standoffish until she knows you better!

Usually sleeps on the bed.

Takes short bursts of energetic exercise, then sleeps for hours!

KREMLIN

Here is a cat with aristocratic blood. Kremlin's mother was a pedigree Russian Blue, hence his name. His looks reveal his breeding: he has the large, pointed ears and luminous, well-spaced green eyes of the Russian Blue. His placid temperament is also a hallmark of the breed, likewise his long, elegant legs and strong, muscular body.

NIGHT-WALKER

Kremlin likes to sleep anywhere except in his own personal basket! He hates being shut in, and prefers to go out at night and sleep during the day.

CLEVER CAT

Kremlin's cleverest trick is retrieving little balls of paper which he persuades people to throw for him. He seeks them out, carries them back and waits for them to be thrown again - just like a little dog!

CATERISTICS

🐾

Fascinated by water, prowling precariously around the bathtub.

🐾

Extremely charming, but can be a little aloof.

🐾

Tolerates canned food, but prefers fresh fish.

BIG SOFTIE

Although he is considerably larger than many cats, Kremlin is gentle, easy-going and quick to make friends with other cats.

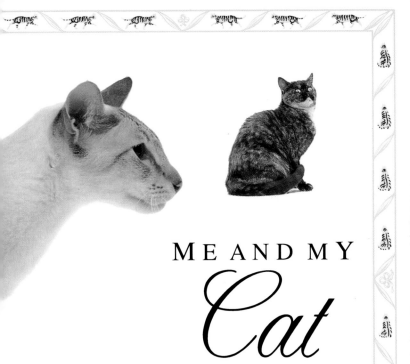

ME AND MY
Cat

*A personalized guide to
choosing the perfect name,
interpreting the sun sign
and charting the individual
achievements of your
tabby cat.*

MY CAT'S PURR-SONAL HISTORY

My cat's name ....

Date of birth ....

Birthplace ....

Weight ....

Sun sign ....

Color of eyes ....

Color of coat ....

Distinguishing features..

Mother and father (if known) ....

Brothers and sisters ....

MY CAT'S FAVORITE THINGS

Gastronomic goodies ....

Napping spots ....

Cat-tricks and games ....

Special stroking zones..

Main scratching post ....

*T*HE FIRST TIME MY CAT...

Opened its eyes ....

Drank a saucer of milk ....

Ate solid food ....

Sat on my lap and purred ....

Said "Meow!" properly ....

Understood the point of kitty litter ....

Presented its first mouse-gift ....

Got stuck in a tree ....

Tried to climb into the bathtub ....

Met a strange cat ....

Fell in love ....

Ran up the curtains ....

Saw a dog ....

Smelled catnip ....

Used body language ....

Used the cat-flap ....

Went exploring outdoors ....

NAMES AND NAMING

"The Naming of Cats is a difficult matter," wrote T. S. Eliot in *Old Possum's Book of Practical Cats*. He didn't make it any easier by suggesting that cats should have "three different names": one "the family use daily", one that's "more dignified", and one known only to the cat, a "deep and inscrutable, singular Name". Nevertheless, the following suggestions may solve the problem for you!

BAGHDAD   *The shimmering, stripy silk fabric known in Victorian England as "tabby" had its origins in Baghdad.*

BESS   *For a tabby with blotched markings, first seen in England during the reign of Queen Elizabeth I.*

CYPRUS   *A "Cyprus cat" is a rustic name for a tabby, but the origins of its usage are unknown.*

DAWN-DAPPLE   *For a pretty puss whose coat is early-morning gray with soft blotches of black.*

EGYPT   *The aristocratic creatures staring out from ancient wall-paintings are the distinguished forebears of today's tabby.*

FRANCOIS   *After the evil, brooding cat in Zola's spine-chilling novel,* Thérèse Raquin, *who would stare intently at the plotting lovers with his huge green eyes, "lost in a kind of devilish ecstasy".*

JENNYANYDOTS   *One of T. S. Eliot's "Practical Cats", she had "a coat of the tabby kind with tiger stripes and leopard spots", who "sits and sits and sits and sits".*

LOTTO *An Italian painter who portrayed a tabby cat in his work.*

MACKEREL *For a tabby with the classic neat black stripes on its coat.*

MICETTO *An ecclesiastical tabby who belonged to Pope Leo XII and as a kitten was carried in a fold of the papal sleeve.*

MISS TABBY *A fairytale cat who, having enraptured a man with her beauty, turned herself into a woman in order to marry him. But on their wedding night, reverting to type, she leaped out of bed in hot pursuit of a mouse, and instantly became a tabby again.*

PINKIEBOY *A favorite tabby of celebrated British gardener Gertrude Jekyll, he had a white bib and paws and impeccable manners.*

TIGER *The natural name for a wonderfully striped tabby cat.*

CAT SUN SIGNS

Check out your cat's sun sign and pick a compatible pet.

ARIES
MARCH 21 - APRIL 20

Adventurous creatures, Aries cats are not restful pets. Although fiercely independent, they have a very loyal streak, and adore being fussed over when in the right mood. *LIBRAN owners lavish attention on the egocentric Aries cat; AQUARIAN owners like the Aries cat's straightforward approach to life.*

TAURUS
APRIL 21 - MAY 21

The Taurean puss is always purring and is happiest when asleep on its favorite bed. Taureans love food and, not surprisingly, tend to be rather plump. Placid and easy-going, they react fiercely if angered. *VIRGOAN owners create the home Taurean cats love; PISCEAN owners are relaxed by Taurean cats.*

GEMINI
MAY 22 - JUNE 21

An out-and-about cat that gets restless if expected to be a constant, lap-loving companion. An incurable flirt, the Gemini cat's lively nature makes for fascinating, sometimes exasperating, company. *SAGITTARIAN owners share the Gemini cat's need for challenge; VIRGOAN owners won't restrict Gemini cats.*

Cancer
JUNE 22 - JULY 22

Ideal for someone who spends a lot of time at home, the Cancer cat will be constantly at your side, climbing on to your lap at every opportunity. But tread carefully: Cancer cats are easily offended. CAPRICORN *owners suit the Cancer cat's desire for stability;* TAUREAN *owners give Cancer cats security.*

Leo
JULY 23 - AUGUST 23

King or queen of the household, Leo cats must rule the roost unchallenged. They have a striking appearance and keep their coats in shape. They adore praise and will go out of their way to attract attention. CANCER *owners like Leo cats taking charge;* ARIAN *owners enjoy the Leo cat's acrobatics.*

Virgo
AUGUST 24 - SEPTEMBER 22

"Take no risks" is this cat's motto. Intelligent thinkers, Virgoan cats don't mind if their owner is out all day and love a change of scene or a trip in the cat basket. SCORPIO *owners complement the Virgoan cat's inquisitive nature;* GEMINI *owners have an independence Virgoan cats respect and encourage.*

LIBRA
SEPTEMBER 23 - OCTOBER 23

You can't pamper this sensuous feline too much. Librans crave attention, are quick to take offense and don't take kindly to being unceremoniously shooed off a comfy chair. *ARIAN owners are good foil for tranquil Libran cats;* CAPRICORN *owners make the Libran cat feel snug and secure.*

SCORPIO
OCTOBER 24 - NOVEMBER 24

Passionate, magical cats with a magnetic presence. Leaping and bounding with immense *joie de vivre*, the Scorpio cat doesn't usually make friends easily but, once won over, will be your trusty ally for life. *PISCEAN owners share the Scorpio cat's insight;* TAUREAN *owners entice the Scorpio cat back to base.*

SAGITTARIUS
NOVEMBER 23 - DECEMBER 21

Freedom-loving rovers, Sagittarian cats lack the grace of other signs. Their great loves in life are eating and human company, but too much fuss makes them impatient. *LEO owners like the Sagittarian cat's brashness;* AQUARIAN *owners are intrigued to see what the Sagittarian cat will do next.*

CAPRICORN
DECEMBER 22 - JANUARY 20

Unruffled and serene, Capricorn cats are rather timid with strangers. They crave affection but may feel inhibited about demanding it. Be sensitive to their needs. *CANCER owners like the settled existence which Capricorn cats love; GEMINI owners offset the Capricorn cat's tendency to get stuck in a rut.*

AQUARIUS
JANUARY 21 - FEBRUARY 18

Unpredictable, decorative and rather aloof, admire your Aquarian cat from a distance. Inquisitive, this cat rarely displays affection for humans, but observes them with interest. *LIBRAN owners understand an Aquarian cat's feelings; SAGITTARIAN owners share the Aquarian cat's unemotional approach.*

PISCES
FEBRUARY 19 - MARCH 20

Home is where the Piscean cat's heart is. The lure of the garden wall holds no attraction for these cats. Attention centers on their owners, who can be assured of a Piscean puss's single-minded devotion. *LEO owners find Piscean cats entertaining; SCORPIO owners have a dreaminess Piscean cats find irresistible.*

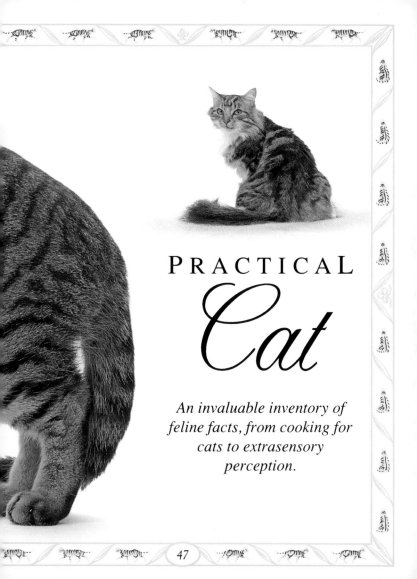

PRACTICAL
Cat

*An invaluable inventory of
feline facts, from cooking for
cats to extrasensory
perception.*

CHOOSING A KITTEN

Choosing a kitten is great fun - but before your
new friend agrees to move in, she will
want to know the answers to a few questions!

WHICH KITTEN?

Persians are luscious, but do you
have time to spend on grooming?
Are you happy to pamper a
pedigree, or do you want an easy-
going cat with an independent
streak? Should kitty be prepared
to spend time alone? Does
neutering fit in with your ideals;
if not, can you cope with the
consequences? If you
decide on a pedigree,
go to a recognized
breeder.

For a non- pedigree, try a cat-
rescue society. It is best to avoid
pet stores.

When you come to choose a kitten, it is wise to bear the following pointers in mind:

1 Choose the brightest, sassiest kitten of the litter.

2 Look for clear eyes, clean ears and nose, sound white teeth and no signs of a tummy upset.

3 Make sure the fur is glossy and healthy, with no fleas, skin problems or blemishes.

4 Check that your kitten is lively and inquisitive, running and jumping with ease, eager to play.

5 Don't take kitty home under ten weeks old.

6 Check that necessary vaccinations have been given.

HOMECOMING

Bring your kitten home in a sturdy box. Give her lots of love, play with her, and don't rush her if she's shy at first. She'll need a warm bed, a litter tray that's regularly cleaned, and her own bowls for food and water. Let her have a good look around before she meets any other household pets. It may take her a while to feel at home, but you will know she's decided to stay when she leaps on to your lap with a contented purr!

TINY KITTENS
Delightful tabby kittens, just four weeks old.

CAT-CHAT

Cats are consummate communicators. They use every part of the body, with subtle vocal variations, to make themselves understood. Here is a guide to demystifying feline bodytalk.

TAIL TALK

- A straight tail with a slight bend at the tip means, "This looks most interesting."
- A tail held stiffly at right-angles to the body means, "Hello. How nice to see you."
- A tail with a tip that twitches means, "I'm starting to get angry!"
- A tail waved vigorously from side to side means, "You're for it!"
- An arched tail with the fur fluffed means, "This is my territory and don't you forget it!"
- A tail held low with fur fluffed out means, "I'm frightened." A terrified cat will crouch down low and the fur will stand on end all over his body.

TONES OF VOICE

- Purring can mean, "Mmmmm, that feels wonderful," or, "You're my favorite person." However, cats have been known to purr when in pain or distress.

- A little chirping sound, which mother cats use to marshal their kittens together, is given by adult cats to say "Hi" to their owners.
- Yowling and caterwauling usually mean, "Get off my territory," rather than, "What are you doing tonight, gorgeous?"
- Hissing and spitting mean, "Get off my patch of ground, or else." These noises may have originated with wild cats imitating the sound of an angry snake.

TRUE TABBY

A loving look when implies complete trust.

BODY LANGUAGE

- Rubbing the body or head against an object is a way of marking territory. When kitty rubs lovingly round your legs, he is saying, "You're all mine."
- A cat with his ears back flat on to his head is saying, "Help!"
- An arched back, with straight legs, wide, staring eyes and electric-shock tail means, "Back off there, or I'll attack!"

- The cat who greets you by rolling lazily over on to his back, presenting his furry underside for you to admire, is saying, "I feel completely safe with you." Don't be tempted to tickle that fluffy tummy: most cats find the area very sensitive, and are likely to react with a reproving paw-swipe.

CELEBRATION CUISINE

Tsar Nicholas I of Russia fed his cat, Vashka, a celebratory concoction of the best caviar poached in rich champagne, with finely minced French dormouse, unsalted butter, cream, whipped woodcock's egg and hare's blood. Rather than trouble his servants, Doctor Johnson himself purchased oysters for his cat, Hodge. It's not necessary to go to *quite* these lengths on those special days when you want to lavish a little more affection on your puss, but here are some gastronomic goodies which will tempt the fussiest feline.

KITTY VOL-AU-VENT

Spoon a dainty, puss-sized portion of cooked chicken and creamy sauce into the pastry case. Top with shrimp for extra-special appeal. Full of protein and vitamins.

LIVER AND BACON BONANZA

Top kitty's portion with crumbled cheese and serve warm. Packed with essential vitamins, minerals and proteins, this is a guaranteed gastronomic success.

Puss's Shrimp Cocktail

Fresh shrimps on delicate slivers of brown bread, thinly spread with butter and diced into feline-sized mouthfuls. Elegant and full of energy-giving goodness.

Drink To Me Only

Not all cats like drinking milk. Make sure there's always an adequate supply of water for your puss. Or try a tempting sip of evaporated milk, or even milky, lukewarm tea.

Mackerel Puss Pate

A dessertspoonful of mackerel pâté on fresh fingers of toast makes an instant treat for the fish-loving feline. Rich in protein and Vitamin A.

Tuna Treat

Tuna, in oil or brine, topped with crumbled cheese and grilled lightly makes a well-balanced, heart-warming feast for your feline.

Rare Treat

Raw steak or ground meat, fresh from the butcher's and finely chopped, is a special occasional food for your cat. But be careful not to overdo the raw meat content of your cat's diet.

Sweet Puss

Cats can be partial to cantaloupe, the occasional segment of apple, or even the odd sweet grape. Full of essential, health-giving Vitamin C and dietary fiber.

CAT GLAMOUR

If you are the proud owner of a Persian cat, it's essential to give your pet a daily grooming session. Shorthaired cats are better at looking after their coats, so a good brush-and-comb once or twice a week is all that is really necessary.

CARING FOR THE FACE
For the eyes and ears, clean carefully with Q-tips soaked in a warm, weak solution of baking soda.

GROOMING THE FUR

1 *Work grooming powder into the coat. For best results, always make sure it is evenly distributed.*

2 *Brush the fur upwards, all over the body, to remove any trace of tangles and dirt.*

Fur On The Face

This can be brushed gently with a toothbrush, but be careful to stay well away from the eye area.

Tooth Care

Check the teeth for tartar build-up and if necessary clean with a toothbrush and a baking soda solution.

3 Add the finishing touches by brushing the fur vigorously all over the body.

4 Shorthaired cats can be given extra shine by rubbing the coat over with velvet, silk or chamois.

A-Z of Cat Care

A IS FOR **ACCIDENT**
Laws protecting injured cats vary from state to state. Keep your pet off the street. Indoor cats live longer, safer lives.

B IS FOR **BASKET**
Useful for traveling, although harder to clean than plastic carriers. Line with paper towels. Do not leave puss inside for too long.

C IS FOR **CAT-FLAP**
Use only where outdoors is safe. Fit at cat's-belly height and make sure it can be locked securely.

D IS FOR **DOG**
Cats tolerate dogs' presence in the same household and can form lasting canine friendships if they are introduced in early kittenhood.

E IS FOR **EXERCISE**
There is cat furniture for exercising. Cat trees can be built. Cats flex their muscles in boisterous play sessions with their owners. A few can even be trained to walk on a leash.

F IS FOR **FLEA COLLAR**
Put one on puss every summer, before he starts scratching. Check that it fits and does not rub.

G IS FOR **GRASS**
Cats love to eat and regurgitate it, along with any hairballs. Indoor cats should be given a pot-grown clump to graze on.

H IS FOR **HANDLING**
Most cats adore a cuddle, but pick puss up gently and support his whole weight. Don't grab him by the scruff or hold him under the front legs without a steadying hand under his rear.

I IS FOR ILLNESS AND INJECTIONS

Feline Infectious Enteritis and Pneumonitis are the two big - but preventable - dangers. Have your cat vaccinated at around 12 weeks old and remember to arrange booster shots. Reputable catteries will not accept cats for board without certificates showing proof of vaccination.

J IS FOR JACOBSON'S ORGAN

Cats occasionally make a strange "grimacing" facial expression, with the lip curled back, when specific smells such as catnip waft past. They are making use of Jacobson's Organ, an extremely refined sense of smell which responds delightfully to certain triggers.

K IS FOR KEEPING STILL

Something a cat can do to perfection, but never when you are trying to administer medicine! Liquids or crushed pills can be added to food. Or grasp the cat's head and bend back gently until the mouth opens. Press on each side of the mouth to increase the gap, and pop the medicine on the tongue as far back as you can. Close the mouth until the cat swallows. Check to make sure the medicine really has gone down.

L IS FOR LITTER TRAY

Keep in a quiet place. Make sure it is always clean and neat. If not, puss may object and then decide to perform elsewhere.

M IS FOR MOVING

Keep kitty under lock and key while the move takes place. When you arrive, let him settle in gradually, a room at a time. Much safter to keep puss inside until you're sure he has settled down.

N IS FOR NEUTERING

Male kittens should be neutered at eight - ten months; females at five - six months.

O IS FOR OBEDIENCE

Start young, and be persistent. Say "No" firmly, as you pluck puss off the forbidden chair and he'll soon start to cooperate - at least while you're within eyesight.

P IS FOR POISONOUS PLANTS

Avoid the following: azalea, caladium, dieffenbachia, ivy, laurel, philodendron, poinsettia, solanum capiscastrum, or keep out of cat's reach.

Q IS FOR QUARANTINE

Holiday romances can have costly consequences, as the holidaymakers who fell for a Portuguese cat found out. The cost of quarantine for six months exceeded $2000.

R IS FOR RODENT

Cats hunt for sport rather than for nourishment, so be sure to feed your cat well if you want the local mouse colony decimated - a ravenous cat lacks the necessary energy and enthusiasm for exhausting pursuits!

S IS FOR SAFETY

Guard open fires; ban cats from the kitchen when ovens and hotplates are on and store sharp knives safely; unplug electrical appliances where cats might chew the cord; keep upstairs windows closed or inaccessible; lock up household poisons and keep the garage closed; beware when using irons; tidy away tiny objects that could choke.

T IS FOR TOYS

The best are often the simplest and it is not difficult to create the most entertaining playthings from the very simplest of materials: a cork swinging from a string, an empty box to hide in, a ping-pong ball, an old spool of thread, a felt mouse for pouncing practice, an old newspaper to stalk - it's quite simply a question of using the imagination, since the list is endless!

U IS FOR UNMENTIONABLE HABITS

Unneutered toms create the most pungent of smells when they mark out their territory. Even if your pets are neutered, you may need to discourage local toms from visiting via your cat-flap and leaving their overpowering mark.

V IS FOR VET

If puss has a prolonged stomach upset, seems lethargic, starts sneezing or coughing, looks rheumy-eyed (the inner eyelid may be showing), or shows signs of pain when handled, ignore any protests and whisk him to the vet straight away. Vets can also advise on vaccinations and booster shots.

W IS FOR WORMS

Most cats suffer now and then. Pills are the answer - your vet can advise on this.

X IS FOR XTRA-SENSORY PERCEPTION

Experts argue that cats have no sixth sense, but anyone who observes a cat bristle in response to something unseen by human eyes will be less convinced.

Y IS FOR YOUNG CATS AND KITTENS

Enjoy their antics while they are playful babies. All too soon they will become more sedate and self-conscious, and will save their displays of tail-chasing or shadow-stalking for moments when they think you're not looking.

Z IS FOR ZOO

Watch out for the African and European Wild Cats, the closest relatives of the average domestic puss. There is a distinct and uncanny resemblance between a tame, snoozing tabby cat and a slumbering tiger: these and other fearsome breeds, like lions and leopards, feature on a more distant branch of the family tree.

I N D E X

ACKNOWLEDGEMENTS

PAGE 10 - The Cat and Mouse in Partnership by Arthur Rackham / Mary Evans Picture Library.

PAGE 11 Puss in Boots by Warwick Goble / Mary Evans Picture Library; "Pussy Cat, Pussy Cat, where have you been?" by Willy Pogany / Mary Evans Picture Library.

PAGE 12 The Thirsty Kitten by Alice Mary Havers / Fine Art Photographic Library Ltd.

PAGE 13 Wisteria Cat (detail) by Ditz / The Bridgeman Art Library; A Fly on the Wall (detail) by B. Cobb / Fine Art Photographic Library Ltd.

PAGE 14 Fritz the Cat / The Kobal Collection.

PAGE 15 A Pampered Pet / Fine Art Photographic Library; The Kitten (detail) by Ditz / The Bridgeman Art Library.

PHOTOGRAPHY: Dave King   **ILLUSTRATIONS:** Susan Robertson, Stephen Lings, Clive Spong